ALL THE STARS THAT FILLED MY SCARS

A COLLECTION A POETRIES

TARJANI GAJJAR

Made with ♥ on the Notion Press Platform
www.notionpress.com

MY REGARDS TO YOU!

To my parents & brother, whose love has been the guiding light

To my two cherished friends, who stood by me through the
darkest of times

And to my mentor, whose faith in me ignited my spirit and
provided support during the hardships of my life

Contents

Contents

Contents

Preface

Being a teenager is a roller coaster ride of troubles and amusements, simultaneously exciting and scary!

In these pages, I share the transformational journey of a girl much like any other – lively, sociable, and emotional. But life had its plans, throwing her into a whirlwind of events that reshaped her entirely.

Through adversity, she emerged as a wiser, more resilient version of herself. The trials she faced taught her the importance of self-love and emotional intelligence, transforming her from an extroverted chatterbox into a stoic, yet internally vibrant, introvert...

1. What's it like, to be yourself?!

"Why aren't you like other girls?" they inquire
Expecting diamonds, pearls, and attire to inspire
"You were born so lovely, so slim and fair
But where's that beauty fading away, where?"
"Why ignore fashion, why not dress up?
Come on, it's a party, don't be abrupt!
Wear an elegant gown, stop that frown
I don't understand, why turn it down?"
"A lady, polite, sits with grace
One leg crossed, it's commonplace
Why don't you conform, does it chafe?
Refusing the norms! someone's brave."
"You hit the gym, but where's the result?
Yes to salads, no to junk, your answer to insults
Instead of weights, go for a run
You'll shed the pounds, have some fun!"
"What ride do you fancy, Tj, my dear?"
"A bike," I reply, the response sincere
"Oh, be a girl, what's with this whim?"
Gender stereotypes, growing dim

"Forgive my intrusion, my words of late
Your talents shine, I appreciate
Strong, sensible, and witty, you excel
But why Mickey on the t-shirt, not Minnie, can you tell?"

2. An Awful Good Cry

Blurry and woolly my sight is
Is everything fading away?
Nope, they're just my tears
Filled in my eyes
Wanting to fall off and trickle down my cheeks
Wetting them, and the eyelashes and my nose
My glasses make it harder for me to see
I get a burning sensation with an excruciating pain!
Trying to wipe them off
But they are unstoppable
Tired of my monotonous crying
Not knowing what to feel anymore
Just trying to demystify myself to others
But the words remain suppressed
Empathy is what I anticipate
Sympathy is what I get
Look now,
My hair's all messed up
And so am I
But here I am
again,
Out of my room with a smile

Letting myself be hypocritic
and replying

"I am fine! Thank you..."

3. Teen-ult

The tissue whispers softly
"I'll withstand your tears, fear not."
While water murmurs gently
"I'll soothe your sniffles, calm your fraught."
The moonbeams down, a silent embrace
"I'll be your constant, in the night's embrace."
And stars twinkle, a comforting sight
"Your dim moments, they do not define your light."
Coffee's aroma, a nostalgic embrace
Memories brewed, in each warm embrace
Mirror reflects, without a trace of scorn
In your flaws, beauty's born
The wind whispers, a gentle sigh
"Breathe, relax, beneath my sky."
Sunshine promises, a fresh start
Another chance, to heal your heart
Music beckons, an escape unfurled
A companion in a chaotic world
Birds' symphonies, a chorus of peace
Nature's melody, where worries cease
The door stands firm, a friend in rage
"Slam me, release, on life's stage."

Journal pages promise secrets kept
"Confide in me, your fears adept."
Nature's arms, impartial and wide
"Calmness I offer, by your side."
In her embrace, no judgments are known
Just solace, in the seeds I've sown

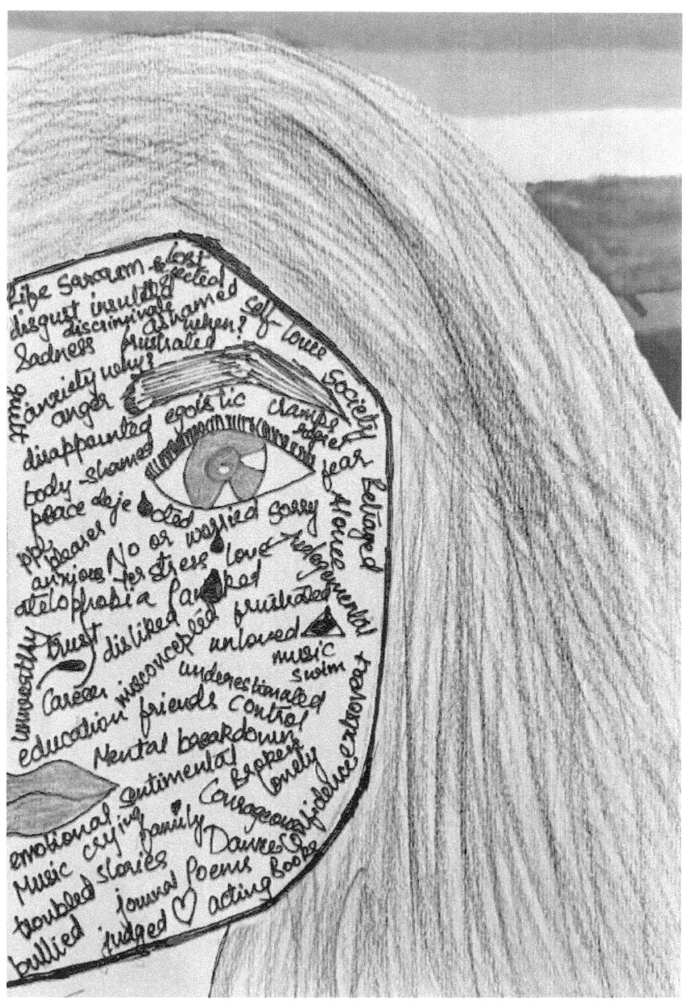

4. Silent Musings

You shed tears when wounded
But what stings deeper
Is the silent cry unnoticed
When no one lends an ear
So spare your kindness for another
For I am unaccustomed to its touch
My heart has grown numb
In the absence of care, it's been left to clutch
I've learned to deal with this world alone
Where tears go unnoticed, unheard
Where pain is a solitary burden
And kindness, a foreign word
So don't offer your sympathy
For my heart has grown to a void
In this world where indifference reigns
My tears have long been destroyed...

5. Nomad For Thy Love

She, who was fed
By the hands of people of her own
Was bitten by the same
She who was unknown of them
Felt like a home around
She, who was a nomad
Seeked nothing,
But thy love…

6. Weight of the Soul: Verses on Gravity

Standing on the ground
I look at the sky, a vault of heaven I must say
The sight of celestial bodies leaves me amazed!
Thereupon I become nostalgic
Reminiscing our time together
I feel worthless, standing there
Alone and hopeless
Your love lifted me!
But I feel
There is no force
To pull me back
From the nostalgic times
You and I had...

7. Through the Miles

In the weary dawning of another day

An unspoken sigh whispers, "Here we go again."

Yet within her beats the heart of a warrior

Resolute, unyielding

She strides forth into the day's embrace

Each dawn a canvas for her to paint

Through the toil of mornings and the weariness of nights

Her soul yearns for an escape

To a city where her name a whisper

In the solitude of her's

She finds the hush of nature's symphony

The weight of yesterdays lifts from her shoulders

As she surrenders to the serenity of the moment

Beneath the canopy of sky and shade

She dips her toes into the cool lake

Where lotuses dance upon the surface

And whispers of ancient tales ripple through the water

With a novel in hand, she loses herself in prose,

"He's more myself than I am;

whatever souls we're made of his & mine are the same"

Each word a refuge
words where love and souls intertwine in eloquent embrace
A smile graces her lips, a ray of sunlight kisses the page
she finds solace
a gentle reminder that
Nature and love remain companions
Refreshed, renewed, she returns from her sojourn
For in the quiet of her journey
She has found the strength to welcome each new dawn with open
arms

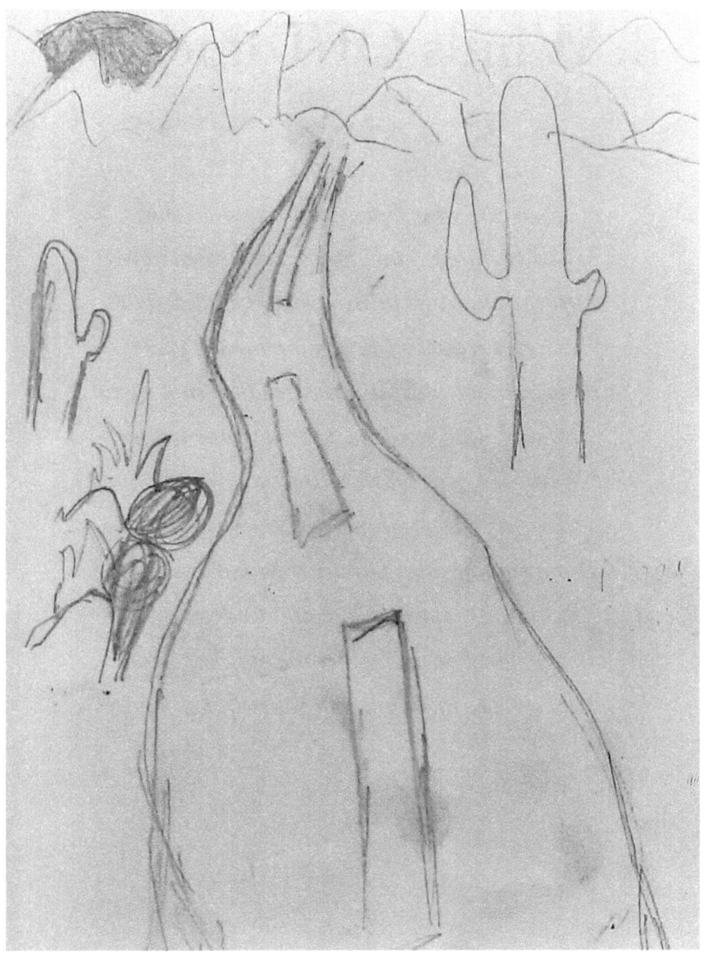

8. Winds Of Tomorrow

Extricate your feelings from deep within
Like a fountain dancing, releasing what's been
Let the past drift away, a river's endless flow
Never retracing, always onward it goes
Be bold in solitude, like the steadfast sun's glow
Radiant and resilient, with a steady tempo
When bruised, seek solace within your own embrace
For self-love outshines any external grace
If you stumble and fall, let tears have their say
But come tomorrow, rise and find your way
Embrace new beginnings, let the old chapters mend
It's time to move on, and yourself, befriend

9. Elixir of My Soul

I look up
I see a silver object risen
Gleaming-white
In the fresh dark sky…
Its arrival is untroubled and effortless!
It has no intention of carrying, but
To make the night alive!
Thereby my soul shows its ardency
As it isn't recognised in the light…
The ethereal glow of its'
Wakes up the longing desire!
The mind is dubious to speak up
As it is the one asleep…
The mischief of shooting stars
Arouses the heart
Making me a reverie
A gust of cold wind flows
Through the room
Through me
It touches my soul…
It is not just the coldness
That regales me

It is the fragrance of his soul
Along with the lush green plants
And the flashbacks
Filled with times
Times that changed me for the better!
I'd always seen him
As a paradisiacal body
As his existence made me wanna wake up…
The night
Assures me
That he existed…
I feel grateful
For he lives!
Yet the heart lives shattered
Not because I don't own him
But because he doesn't own me!
He was just the right person
At the wrong time!
It is memories like these
Which makes me wanna believe
In love
So what if I wasn't bestowed with his love
But I still carry his memories within me…
Just so for my soul
To fulfil its long desire!

10. Forlorn Wanderings

Dried-up grass around me
As tall as me
I can see in the darkness
Moon fading away
I see the sun in a while
But no rays
It seems as if someone has lifted their brushes
Painted the sky dark-bluish pink
And have added the sun to it
Like a cherry on the cake…
But nature no longer astonishes me
As I accompany the sunrise every day
As I sit with my legs crossed
My hands wrapped up in the pocket of my hoody
I take a sigh…of relief
I always thought of myself
To be a 'people-person'
But I guess it was wrong of me
I feel safe around me
Having no one question me
Or anticipating me to be like them
I think I have identified myself

I, just like an old book,
With yellowish-brown pages,
Wrinkled up and torn from some corners
Giving a typical smell…but the content inside
Is still intact
It still gives a vacation to your brain
By letting you go through someone else's shoe
Making you feel like the main character!
Why books?
Perhaps it's the truth been told
By 'Anne-frank' -
"Paper has more patience than people!"
It is pretty grotesque yet relieving
You want to be alone but not lonely
It's merely any pickle to me
It doesn't hurt now
As it has been a chore for me
To withstand the broken words
People to me,
It's like stabbing on the wound,
That already exists…no pain felt
Being forlorn keeps me affiliated
With myself
It keeps me armoured
Against the dreadful war
Between the hearts of the two…

11. Ethereal Moonwake

Amidst the woods, I wander free
my footsteps echo, my breath, a melody
humming softly, as I delve deeper
embracing the shadows, a nature seeker
The darkness here doesn't scare
but draws me in, with its ancient air
a connection blooms with every sound
an artist betwixt life, profound.
I revel in the earth's symphony
crickets' chorus, twigs' harmony
seeking refuge from the biting chill
through the rustling, I find my will
Though the winds resist, I persist
patiently waiting for their fierce twist
jacket shed, I embrace the breeze
observing nature's timeless ease
As the winds relent, the moon takes flight
guiding me through the veils of night
nature's canvas, an endless scroll
each scene is a story, each moment whole
A frozen lake, a sight to behold
ice like glass, a treasure untold

beauty unblemished, pure and rare
I linger, lost in nature's care
Why return home, to walls and strife?
when here, we find nature's life
I find solace, I find my peace
in the woods, my soul's release

12. A Silhouette

Why did you run into me?
If not as a person, but as a shadow
The clouds declutter
The mist clears up
The sun glimmers again
And there you are…
Waving towards me
To come to you
But why should I trust you?
You are just a silhouette!

13. Water's Way

Closing my eyes, I drift away
Loosening my body, I find my way
Relaxed, divine, in tranquil sway
A moment of peace, come what may
A bloop in my ears, water's embrace
Refreshing my face, in its grace
Arms and body, drenched in the chase
Of serenity, in this sacred space
I open my eyes, greeted by blue
Sky above, and horizon anew
Surrounded by ocean's hue
My heart whispers, "Stay, it's true."
I force myself to rise, to flee
But my heart protests, longing to be
In the calm embrace of this sea
Where tranquillity reigns, wild and free

14. Evergreen Meadows

You hold me tight
Take me to the meadows
My hair swirl
You try to look into my eyes
But my hair won't let you
You tuck my hair behind my ears
There…
I look into your eyes
Brown…gorgeous
You take out the canvas
And look at me
Just like a person
Who is awe-struck
By the beauty of the sunset
You pick out colours
White, brown, black and pink…
Your fingers perfectly hold the brush
Calmly and conscientiously
Stroke your hands freely
Letting the pink colour go over the lips
Thereafter you look at me…
In an admiring way!

You let the air dry the paints
Your palms look messy
But they still beautifully hold my hand
You show me the painting
It's image reflected upon my eyes
You ask me how I found it to be
I just let the painting be with me
I wrap my arms around you
Bringing you closer…
We lie on the grass
(green-lushy)
Just been sprinkled with water
The fauna starts to gather around
Ready to enjoy the enthralling sunset
The sky slowly gets painted
Into the shades of red
I scoot myself into you
Your caressing touch
Leaves me unperturbed…
I hold onto the painting
Enjoy the sunset
And cherish us!

15. Left Me As a Ghost

I play the symphonies
Of love on the piano…
But you were never meant
To listen and embrace it!
For me
Playing those notes
Reminded me of you
Just pieces of it…
You wore a shirt,
A mixture of seashell and beige
You used to make me a coffee
Every time…never got the ingredients wrong
(A pinch of cinnamon on the top)
We were bibliophiles
You always read me
The poems from
'The Prophet'
Your words
Made my soul joyful
But with you gone
…I am just a ghost now

16. Superficial

I tried hating you
And loving myself
But how did I end up
Hating myself!
And yet being in love with you?

17. An Echo Chamber

"Hello, is anyone listening?
Or am I merely conversing with myself
Lost in the labyrinth of my mind?"
I see my thoughts ricocheting
Echoing off the walls of this room
Only to rebound back to me
And there I stand
Trapped in the familiar confines of my personality
In two years
A fragment of myself has slipped away
And I yearn for its return
Surrounded by a number of faces
I find myself in a sea of voices
Yet my own words feel hollow
As if they dissolve into the air, unheard
I shout my truths into the void
But they dissipate into the silence of my mind
When will I rediscover that vibrant soul
So full of life and expression?
For I crave her presence more than ever
Once, being enigmatic was a burden
But now, in the absence of expression

I find solace in the quietude
Realizing that the essence of my being has faded away

18. If Only You'd See the Pain Through my Browns

You capriciously deny
To unwind your feelings
so I spent my nights
In the thoughts of you...
You give me hope
You smile at me
Appealing it is!
But why does it have to fade away
When others are around?
We settle at the same place
But you refuse to share the place
In your heart
I understand... mystery guy huh?!
-No
You are nothing
But a closed book...
I confess
I patiently wait
I fall into you
Again and again

TARJANI GAJJAR

I just can't fathom
Which of the fall
Hurt me the most?!

19. Entangled Hearts

You bought me

A bouquet of roses

I held it

But there were no petals

Just the thorns

Honey…why'd you do this?

Why were the petals

Not meant for me?

The thorns pierced

Pierced through

My heart, the one

That had been shattered before

And yet every piece decided to love you!

20. Scent Of Those Chrysanthemums

I hearken back
To the days
When we went to the Appalachians…
I can see you struggling
To breath
I can hear the footsteps
Yours and mine
As we vigorously climb
I can see a skylark
Accompanying us…
You stop me
By taking my palm in yours
You are sweaty
But I still somehow
Smell your cologne
We sit for a while
Catch our breaths
You thread your fingers
Through those chrysanthemums
But it wasn't just the flowers

TARJANI GAJJAR

The view was mystical
And there we sat
Indulged in each other
Enchanted…

21. Amorous Breath

"Bonjour bien-aime,"

"You vex me
Your presence maddens me
Every breath you take near me
Makes me question your demanding affection
My innocence was taken away
By your intimacy
The way you look at me defies my patience
Of wanting to kiss you
My heart beats inconsistent around you
Why am I being affected?
Why is my expediency fading away?
Your touch
Invokes a burning desire in me
I desire to confide in you
Can we meet
At une galerie d 'art
And embrace our love, mi amor?"

"- Your Cheri"

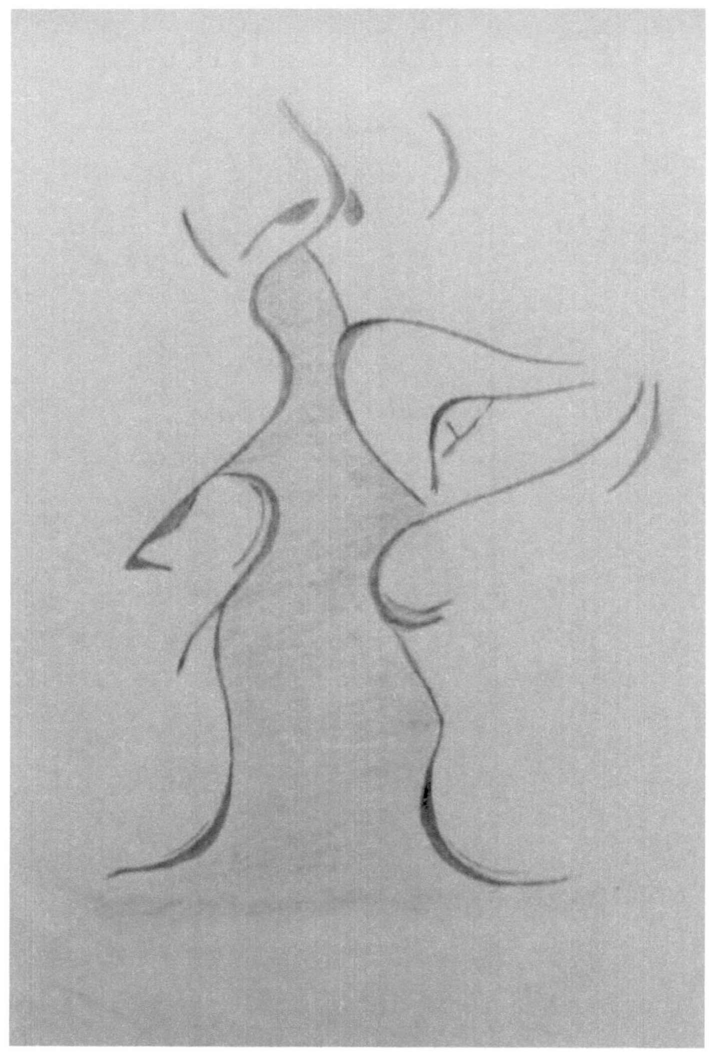

22. Agony

The tears of her
Were like nails on the blackboard
There was darkness for her
Even in a bright sky
She goes on a walk
In a thunderstorm…
Winds rushed against her.
Everyone around her
Running for a shelter
And yet she keeps walking…
She was walking
Into a graveyard
Of dense-menacing clouds
Ready for a downpour
A drop of water
Lands on an orchard
Cuts through the leaf
And falls on her
She no longer
Repress the tears
For she knows
People disregard it…

But for her
The tears had a silver lining

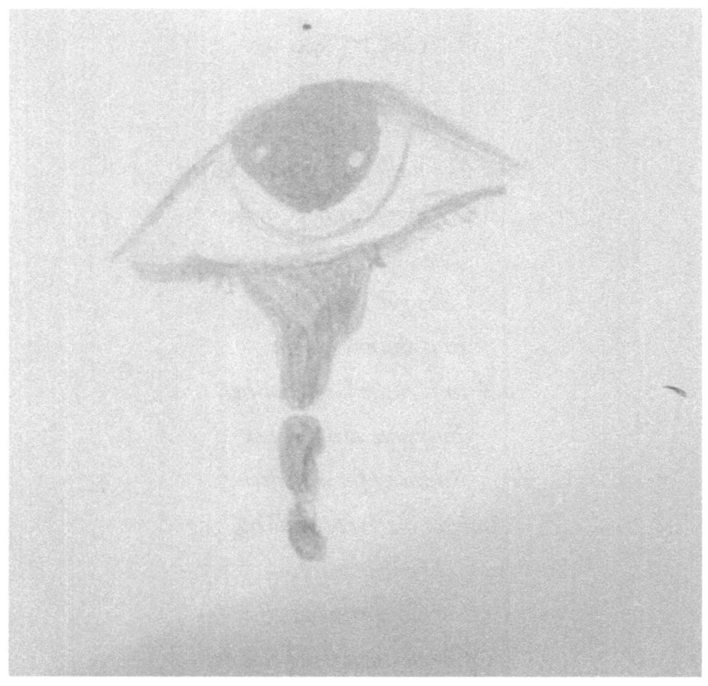

23. A Fallen Star

The sun has risen
The roses have blossomed
And so has our friendship…
If only I could give you a canvas to paint
To your pure, fulfilling and colourful heart
You'd know
How beguiling that piece of art would be!

24. What Have You Done?

You pledged to journey alongside me
Bound together in the same vessel
But now, dear, I find myself adrift
Abandoned on this voyage alone
Your smiles, your gestures, they once
Sufficed to earn my trust
But now, I ought to set sail
Without casting a glance behind
"Such a maverick woman," you'd say
In your attempts to charm
Yet I wasn't the sole admirer
Of your flattering words
With you, I was a polished facade
But now, I'm a merely shattered remnant
Fear not, my love,
I don't lose sleep over you
Nor do I weep at our memories
For you've shown me the shadows
Why do I still carry remnants of you?
- A burden I must bear

You didn't destroy me
But birthed a newer version
I wish you well
In a life veiled in sorrow
Without the presence of me

25. Between Devil and the Deep Blue Sea

If you could cast away this dreary 'now'
And forward through time, to know 'what', 'end', and 'how'?
What would you keep, in your heart's decree
A past's sorrow, or future's mystery?
"The past, a haunt, with its painful weight
Yet in the future, there lies a fate
To erase the past, a tempting thought
But without it, would my path be sought?"
In the echoes of time, she ponders
Between past and future, her mind wanders
For in each moment, a story unfurls
A story woven of pearls and pearls
To forget the present, a tempting plea
But each moment holds its decree
Through pain and joy, life's dance we weave
In the past, present, and future, we believe

26. A Letter To Heaven

I remember the time
When you and I gazed at the stars together
Stared at the paintings of Claude Monet
I wanted to hold you
Bring you closer
Feel your heart
Hug you tightly
And let you know
That everything was going to be just fine
But how could I ever know
That you were suffering
Alone…
While you were smiling at me
While you chose making me happy
I remember the nights
We slept through the cold winters
You kissed my forehead
And let me sleep…
But you were never there
When I woke up
I couldn't hear you anymore
Couldn't feel you anymore

TARJANI GAJJAR

But honey
I'll always love you
And write you letters
Under the same stars
We used to gaze

27. Crowned With Gold Leaves

She was bruised and scarred
She was bleeding
She could see an army of knights with lances in their hands
Coming for her…her empire, her people
She could hear the laments
Of those who had lost their loved ones
She watched women being beaten
She was eying for her empire to fall
She had two choices
To fight or to surrender to those fierce combatants…
It wasn't just her life in jeopardy but of thousands of them
And there…
She swore to the people of hers'…out of belligerence
She took out the sword off the scabbard
She was astride, upon the horse
She pulled the reins and tried hastening up the horse
She slaughtered the savages, fought for her empire
Set free the slaves and saved the dignity of the women
Yet after this bravery, she had been perished
After fighting until her last breath

And her resurrection was awaited!

28. A Melted Chocolate Near The Water

Just wanna be on that bench…some more
Just wanna read your letter again and again…some more
Just wanna keep clicking our pictures…some more
Just wanna talk, with moon smiling at us…some more
Just wanna eat the melted chocolate with you…some more
Just wanna let the wind play with my hair…some more
Just wanna confide in you…some more

"Friend: His appreciation of your presence really got to
you, huh?
You: Yeah, it meant a lot. His words weren't fancy, but his
eyes and smile said it all.
Friend: Now that things are good, you can love him
without worrying he'll leave.
You: Exactly! Our love shines bright, like the moonlight!
(Time passes)
You: Hey, I'm hurting so much. My eyes can't stop crying.
Friend: What happened?
You: I just wanted us to be close. I'm ready to give my all,
but he wants space. I wanted us to go to the meadows, to

*that special pond with lilies just for us. But now, it's like
I'm alone in those meadows, watching the petals fall.
Friend: It's tough. But your care for him remains, right?
You: Yeah, it's like it's stuck there, in those lilies and in the
moonlight on the water...but hey the bond of our
friendship never faded...it still remains!"*

29. Vulnerability: Emotions in the Silence of Mine

Enveloped in conceit and shallowness
That was your guise
Yet your sentiments towards me
Rendered me defenceless in your presence

I lingered, hopeful
As summers faded into winters
But my warmth for you went unnoticed
All that remains to forewarn you
Is the impending moment
When you'll find yourself submerged
Drowning in the depths
Of emptiness, regret, and sorrow
With no guiding hand
To rescue you from those icy depths

30. November Reverie

As dusk descends, painting the sky in shades of black
The chill of night envelops us in its cold

There I stand beside you
Clutching a letter in one hand and a rose in the other
The letter, filled with my essence
Carries the scent of my perfume
Exotic, aromatic, and strong fragrance

Within its pages, a message awaits
Of my enduring and boundless love for you!

31. Chronicle Of the Greens

Oh, those captivating beautiful eyes
That radiant smile that lights up the skies
Your laugh, so carefree and bold
How I wish its echoes, could forever hold
Your words, once a symphony of delight
Now haunt my thoughts, shattering the night
I believed your soul to be pure and true
But beneath the surface, doubt of mine grew
Perhaps your intentions were not malice-laden
But each blow inflicted, left my heart saddened
The transiency of your feelings, just like that of a breeze
My love for you burned with enduring intensity
Fooled once, twice, and now thrice...it seems
My cries of anguish were lost in silent screams
They speak of true love, eternal and divine
Yet you came out to be a lone shadow in a flock so fine

32. Hot Springs of Water

In the forest we were, where the trees rejoiced
As the birds sang melodies, their hearts voiced
Water danced with the wind in euphoria's sway
Nature's symphony in the light of day
And in that moment, our lips puckered, soft and pink
Like petals of a rose, in love's sweet brink
A union of souls, in passion's embrace
Felt the harmony of nature's grace
So let the trees rejoice, the birds in song
As our love blooms, tis where we belong

In the whispers of the wind, rivers' flowed
In this timeless dance, our hearts glowed

I
YOU

33. Torment

Do not walk away, love
It is not forever yet
The words you spoke
Hurt me as much
As swords do!

34. Beyond The Horizon

Take my hand, my love, and let us flee
From the shadows that bind, set ourselves free
17 years of sorrow and despair
Trapped in a cage, a burden too heavy to bear
Why should I board another's sinking ship?
When I know their fate, the water's grip
They wait for me, hoping I'll drown
But with you by my side, I'll wear no frown
I weep for myself, for the loneliness I feel
For the abandonment that seems all too real
But now you're here, my beacon of light
To lead me away from the endless night
Honey, take my hand, be my guide
Lead me to safety, away from the tide
Hold my tears, for they're precious and true
A sign to the pain I've been through
Kiss me as I confide in you, a gentle chase
As we escape to a better place
In your arms, so strong and warm
I feel sheltered from every storm
Turn the helm, my love, to the setting sun
Where the waves dance and dolphins run

Where the winds blur out secrets untold
And the waters guide, cold and cold

35. Silence Is My Favourite Sound!

Slamming of doors
Screams of hatred
Fingers pointed at me
There I sit
With my legs crossed
My arms in the pocket
My tears…umm exactly where they belong
I crave to wear my headphones
I crave to rebel
I crave to shout
But only that
My headphones aren't my reality
Being a rebel is what I can't be
I can't shout with my voice broken
No amount of words can fill up my silence
Did I give too much?
Did I trust too much?
Did I betray myself, being fair to you?
Had I drowned in the waters?
I knew I could swim in

36. Ton Eau De Cologne…fantastique!

In strides he enters, a man of the hour
With a portmanteau, his aura in power
Black shirt, beard kempt, he's a sight to behold
A Spartan's gait, a centaur's bold
He asks with grace to share the seat
I nod in agreement, our eyes do meet
His voice resonates, a deep, rich hue,
Confidence, courage, in all that he'd do
His smile stoic, his work a fierce dance
Like a lion hunting, in a wild trance
Infatuation grips, a queen to her king
In his realm, we'd boldly swing.
Not just a prince, but a monarch, strong
His throne awaits, where we both belong
Ready to protect, our empire, our love, our own
As king and queen, together, we've grown

37. Self-Loathing

"Grant Yourself Grace"
Forgive yourself, they say
It's not as monumental as it seems
Embrace gratitude
And within its folds, rediscover yourself
How, you ask?
4 years have passed
With the shattered fragments of me
Always awaiting a glimmer
During my darkness
It's not about gratitude
Nor merely about optimism
It's about me
Every endeavour is tainted with failure
Or abandoned in resignation
You see an angel
But I'm contained by the shadow of a devil
To be truly understood
Is a rare and exquisite gift
Yet it remains but a yearning
True intimacy is a dream

favorite
place
A HUG

38. Holocene Of Desires

Scream out my name
Stop me
From going away from you
I am snatching my heart
Away from you
Would you not fight?
For that heart?
That always loved you…
The flowers
Are sweet smelling again!
The birds
Are ready to chirp again!
My lips
Are ready
To be kissed by you again!
Will you not let it happen?
Will you not let our fingers intertwine…again?

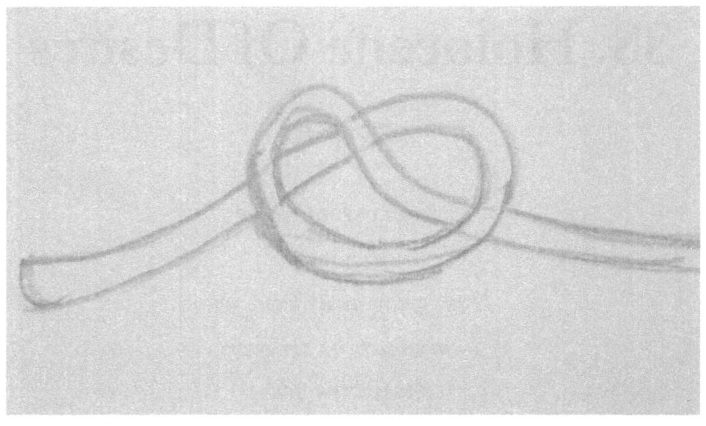

39. An Immortal Traveller

40. Evanesced From Your Life

Red and blue, our palms adorned

Pressed against paper, a pledge sworn

"Always and Forever," the words were read

A vow of eternity lovingly shared

For me, it was an endless bond

While for you, perhaps a chain is too fond

My weakness held close, in sickness and health

You ensured it stayed, my heart's stealth

You, a precious gem, radiant and bright

I reached out, but you took a flight

Deserted, abandoned, left in the cold

Your tears, mere facades, stories untold

I watched you weep...or so I thought

But like a crocodile, your tears were fraught

You moved on, leaving me behind

As I realized, your love was never truly mine

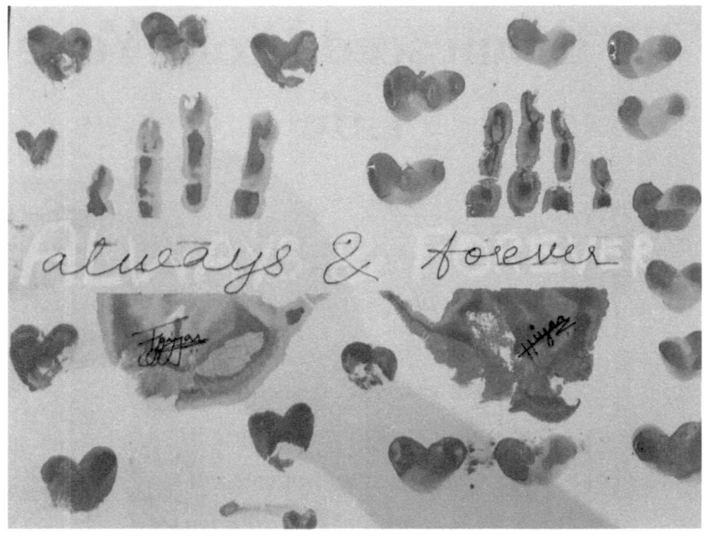
always & forever

41. Night Is Where Our Love Reigns

Void of your absence

The feeble sound of your voice

Those calloused tan fingers

I can feel your breath on my shoulders

I can feel your love, even if you are not here

Why do you not twinkle often?

Let me know if you're still there

Why do you reside during those dark, magical nights?

And not those cold, bright mornings?

Will you guide me to the moon?

Around which you settle

Your gorgeousness is enough for the whole sky

You didn't deserve the selfish land, but the a selfless place up there

Promise me not to fade away…when the sky turns bright

Don't worry darling,

You can rest in peace now!

You'll be gone…but your love will still reign in my heart

42. In My Grave Would You Visit?

Hundreds of shattered pieces
Which are unaware of the blisses
The pages of a novel were torn
For the idea of love was full of scorn
The words on the pages were gone
Just like that, my silence stood there at dawn
The phone never rings
Had I realised it sooner! The awaiting still stings
The heart belongs to all…but beats for one
But the beats were disrupted by the bullet of your gun
My eyes never lie
For they still give a cry
I gulped my wrath
A war between my brain and my heart…was fought!
The one in love always honours
But you treated me like a worthless brawner
My faith in vulnerability was tested
My heart now, has been infected
I no longer feel respected
For my presence for you was neglected

You shan't summon me, not anymore
I implore you…to check your black heart once more!

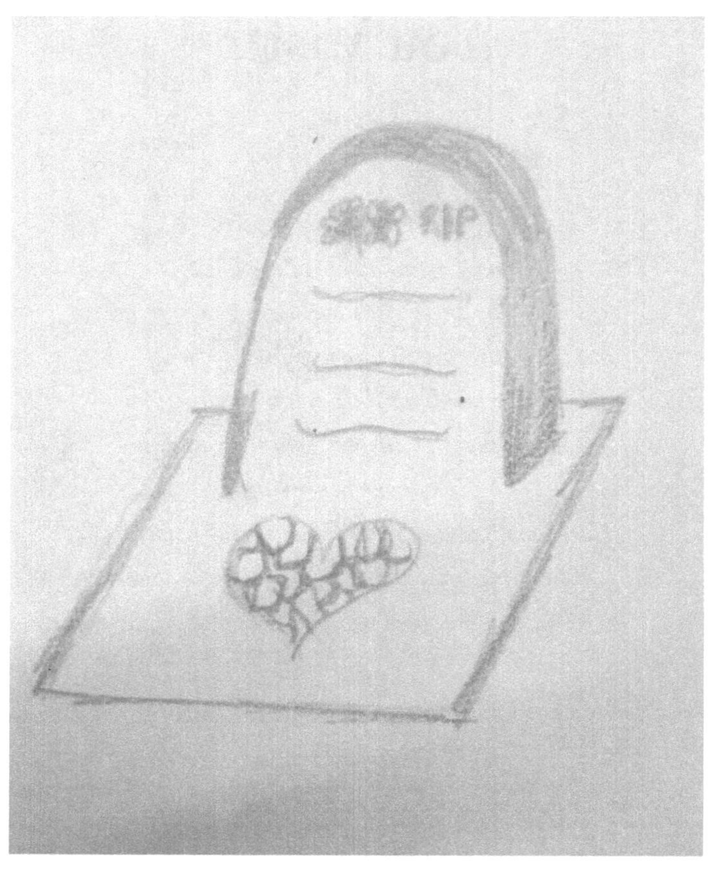

43. Wassail! Drink Hail! A battle to cede, for love…

Pierce my heart

With your love's gentle touch

Be my shield

Protect me from the world's harsh clutch

Come, my dear, with faithfulness

Let your promises never be worthless

Here, take this ring

Place it upon my finger, let our hearts sing

I'll love you as I do myself

Together, we'll defend our fort with wealth

No need for sorrow

Even in battles, we may borrow

For in love's embrace, we've already won

Let's celebrate, for our victory has just begun

44. From Embrace to Farewell

I didn't know,
That smile of yours
Will someday
Be the reason for my tears!

45. A Portrait Of You

Your glamour never phased me
Nor the trends you wear
I see beyond the surface show
To the essence, raw and rare
I could linger on your portrait
Lost in its captivating spell
Each stroke of paint adds
To a beauty, that words can't tell
Your hair, a gentle frame
For a face so softly drawn
No need for laughter to enchant
Your smile, a radiant dawn
In your eyes, a world unfolds
Pupils like freshly minted pearls
Reflecting depths of untold stories
In the ocean where mystery swirls
I may not know your name
Yet it feels strangely serene
To be drawn into your presence
In a moment, a world unseen
But you're but a painting
A vision trapped in art's grace

TARJANI GAJJAR

How can I bridge this distance
To meet you in time and space?

46. To All The Men Who Stood By Me

How do you do it, I wonder
To battle the demons within
While fiercely defending your love?
How do you embody such selflessness?
Such love, such responsibility
When it comes to your kin?
Grieving and laughter entwined
A paradox of emotions
A testament to your resilience
Why is your worth not appreciated enough
As you stand, a pillar of masculinity
Holding this world together?
Why do you choose silence?
When your soul screams in agony
Shattered from within
Yet, with all the chaos
Your dedication shines through
To yourself, to your craft, unwavering
You bring joy to a woman's heart
With your support, your protection

Your steadfast presence
And in the eyes of a mother
Gleams pride untold
As her son grows into his strength
For a woman may possess a tender heart
But yours beats with equal gentleness
Or perhaps, even more ardently

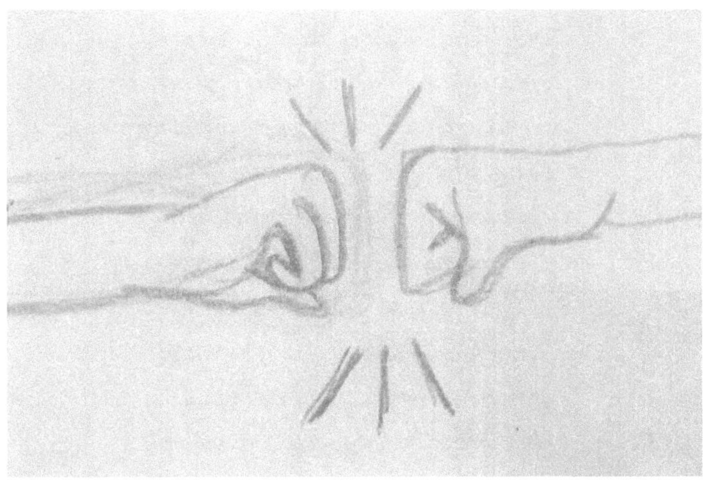

47. Healing The Wounds

In the quest for love, we embark
And so did I, with a hopeful spark
A longing that grips, and makes us yearn
In its fervent flames, we start to burn
He caught my eye in a fleeting glance
An encounter, where we took our chance
Though strangers in name, not in vibe
In that moment, connections arrive
I, pragmatic, in life's daily dance
Once deemed love a mere stance
He, a force, made my thoughts blind
In his presence, a shift I did find
His voice, a melody, soothing and low
I felt no urge to speak, just to listen and know
Not mere desire, but a longing for pure
Each meeting, a craving, seeking more
Love, a potion potent and strong
It eases the hurt but prolongs the song
Yet, this isn't of amour's tales
Rather a wish, in a separate space
A puzzle, to behold one near
Whose feelings for you remain unclear

For he was real, his presence keen
In the realm of emotions, a conundrum scene
Unrequited love, a daunting plight
A struggle to bridge the gap in the sight
What can I do to make him see?
Perhaps only wish, to set love free

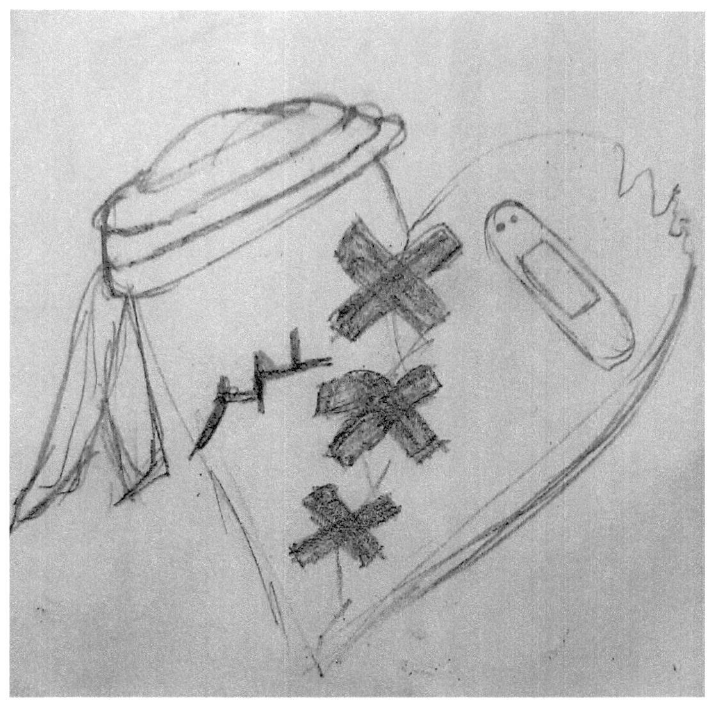

48. Behind The Facade

"Why do you write?"
they ask
Seeking a path
To find the labyrinth of pain
Without the numbing pills, in vain

49. Voluntary Captivation

Take me with you
where the sun never stops shining
where the moon never fades
where the love whispers
the songs that bewitch us
your face is like that of a greek god
unknown to all but me
skin like that of water
lips like that of juicy fruit
the eyes kept shining...immortal elixir
your breath exhaled stars
stars I could keep gazing...

50. Dead of Night

In the depths of night, I'm swallowed whole
My heart rebels, my mind cajoles
A spell of sleep, its gentle call
My heart resists, it wants it all
Enchanted by the moon's soft glow
The stars that twinkle, a celestial show
The breeze, whispers in the dark
Accompanied by the cricket's spark
At this moment, I am torn
Between what's safe and what's adorned
But a choice is made, in quiet might
To sleep in joy, beneath the night's soft light

51. Connoisseur Of Emotions

Isolation, you say?
- Nay, 'tis solitude I embrace
Comfort found in my own space
Not lonely, but content to stay
Why seek the crowd's allure
When solitude offers much more?
In the silence, I find clarity
Away from the world's disparity
How to convey this truth profound
To those who chase the empty sound?
Escaping from reality's grasp
In a facade that's sure to lapse
When asked, "What's up? How do you fare?"
I ponder if they truly care
Disconnected from the charade
In solitude, my soul's unafraid
In the stillness, I discern,
Emotions deep within me churn
Away from the noise, I grow
In solitude, my true self I show

Why the constant need for noise
When does silence hold such poise?
No music, friends, or coffee near
Just me, my thoughts, and nothing to fear
Why forsake the soul's pursuit
For shallow trends and pursuits?
Rather, seek within,
Where authenticity begins
Have we lost our way, I ponder
In a world where noise grows fonder?
Let us be the guides, the seers
Of our own emotions, our frontiers

52. Eschew The Reality

In the quiet of turning pages
And pens that fidget with restless rages
Legs that shake in silent thrall
And eyes, in concentration's call
In this focused scene,
I find myself lost in between,
Faces absorbed in written lore,
Words meant for them, not for my door.
In a reality where I seek to dwell
Fluids rush, a dizzying swell
Aching to burst forth, this painful strain
Eyes tired from the effort to remain
Struggle to speak, to feign a grin
While lips protest each movement within
Questioned about sleep, I offer no reply
Leaving the bed feels like a lie
Content to linger, bed-bound and free
Working, reading, at my own decree
Among the crowd with marked-up sheets
I hold a blank page, empty and neat
Driving away, seeking escape's embrace
I sit in silence, seeking solace's grace

Asked by my Mom, what troubles my mind
I dismiss her concern, stoic and kind
Learning to cloak emotions deep
Sweating outside, while inward, I weep
Home at last, before the mirror I stand
Mastering the art of hidden tears wiped by my hand
For though cheeks ache and jaws may throb
The tears stay dormant, a silent sob
Have I learned to veil my soul's revealing?
Or merely mastered the art of concealing?

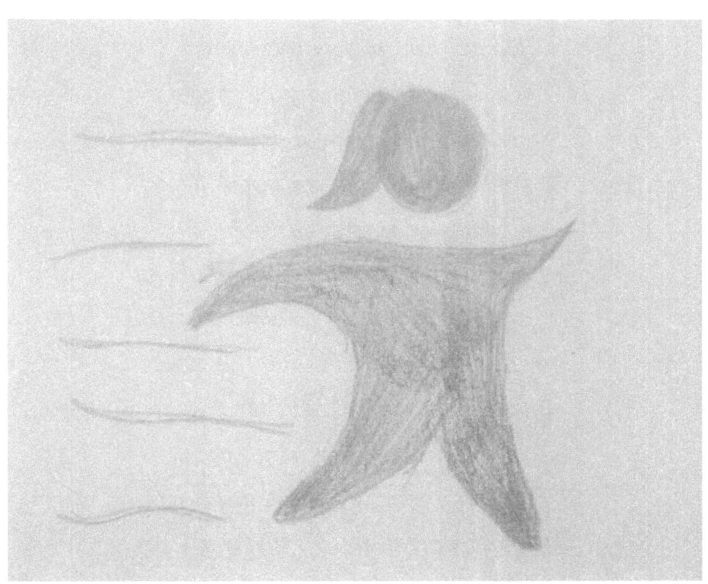

53. Resilience Over Chaos

Promises made, but often broken
Leaving us fractured, words unspoken
Journey, a bittersweet symphony
Lessons learned while in an agony
Struggling for respect, striving to grow
In the depths of darkness, our resilience shows
Melancholy grips, a chosen state
As maturity dawns, priorities dictate
Silent acceptance, a subtle choice
In the cacophony of life's relentless voice

54. All The Stars, That Filled My Scars

Why is it
I fight battles for others
But falter in my defense?
Why do my words flow freely to you
Yet I struggle to be the girl you desire
I sacrificed for you
Only for you to forsake me for another
And still, I yearn for your presence
You promised to be my anchor
As I let myself drift upon the waves
But it wasn't long until I realized
I had drowned in your absence
How is it that you see only my smile
And not the tears hidden in my eyes?
You let me into your world
Loved me, cared for me, shielded me
I placed my trust in you, believed in you
Loved you with all my being
And then... you vanished
Leaving me bereft of a shoulder to lean on

TARJANI GAJJAR

Abandoned in the flames
While I waited, hoping for your return

55. A Coffee Just Sipped

Amidst the chaos, my voice found its grace
Soothing the screams, leaving not a trace
Tears, bold yet shy, refused to descend
Fearing exposure, they chose to pretend
In the depths of my eyes, pain silently dwells
Veiled by a smile, the story it tells
Love, a fleeting companion, left me to stand
Alone with my thoughts, coffee in hand
"Alcohol?" they inquire, seeking a reprieve
But the puzzle of pain, I'm determined to perceive
Feelings linger, unresolved, in the heart's maze
Refusing to fade, in this intricate daze

COFFEE

56. The Day Of Realisation

In the quiet of a room
Within a cosy nook
Curtains were drawn against the day's intrusion
Still slivers of sunlight slip through
Reminding me of the world outside
While I'm engrossed in a digital dialogue
Awaiting a response from someone close
But minutes stretch into hours
And hours into days
A slow realization dawns
The expectations I hold
Are self-imposed, a prison of my own making
Constructed around me, by myself
Is it too late to understand?
To grasp the truth that we're mere mortals
For whom others scarcely spare a thought?
Yet emotions cling, stubbornly
Refusing to yield to reason
Like a guilty party feigning innocence
In the face of undeniable evidence

So I swallow the bitter pill
No longer waiting for their move
But instead, I take the step
To forge ahead, and move on

57. Stitch Me With Your Love

Feel my heart beat as I draw near
Look beyond my facade, clear
As I collapse, holding my form tight
See-through my soul in this endless night
I bleed from wounds, raw and deep
Stitch me up with love, let it seep
Conceal the scars with your tender embrace
Stay with me, in this sacred space
Stitch me together, let me feel
Your touch, your breath, so real
Your fingers, there, with mine
Kisses soft as whispered wine
I feel the scars begin to fade
Healing under love's sweet cascade
But why do you start to drift away?
Can't you linger, in this night's sway?
Stay with me until the scars mend
Until our souls blend
Together, let's heal, forever bound
In love's embrace, where solace is found

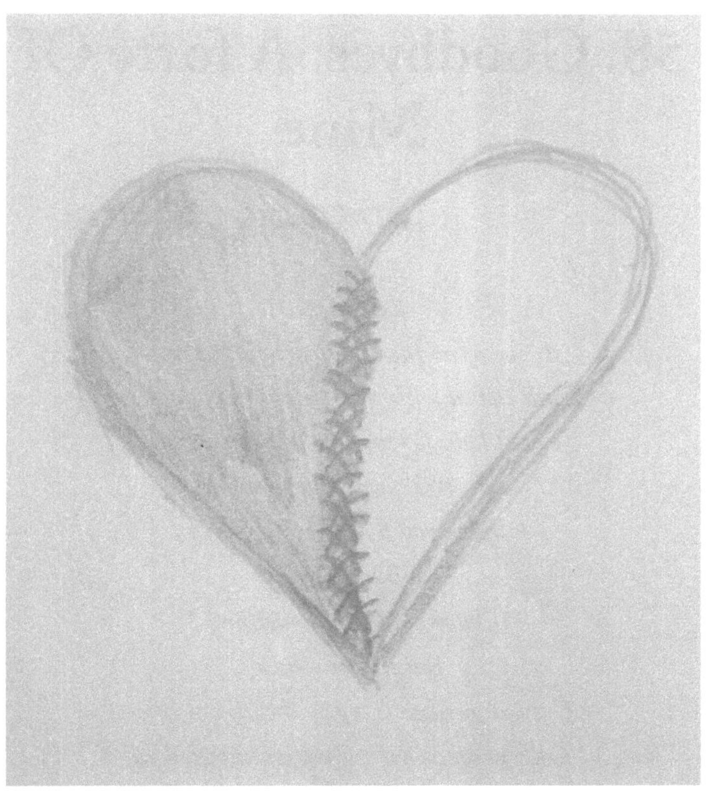

58. Goodbyes: A forte Of Mine

Late night

A ring of notification pierces the silence

Words etched with remorse, with resignation

"I can't fight for you like you did for me."

Efforts limited, love withheld

A thank you for the care bestowed

But wait,

"I have made you something."

But silence echoes

Unread messages hang in the digital ether

Calls unanswered, pleas unacknowledged

Not a bullet, but a sword

Piercing through the armour of love

Blood flows freely, screams rend the night

Tears, like acid, sear the skin

Burning away the facade of strength

Lessons learned

In the crucible of heartache

Hate taught, love weakened

Hearts are not always red but bruised and broken

Alive, yet dead inside
Trust shattered, romance futile
Emotions toyed with
Friendships forsaken
Apologies hollow, sincerity lost
One more lesson sought
How to bid farewell
Without a trace of remorse
In this cruel dance of goodbye

59. A Rising Reign: Girl to a Woman, Ignited the 18th Candle!

From shattered dreams to soaring heights
A journey marked by lonely nights
Once a heart so full of light
Now cloaked in shadows, out of sight
From giving all, to losing ground
Her laughter was lost, and no joy found
Yet through the pain, a strength arose
A phoenix from the ashes, she chose
From outward charm to inner peace
Her turmoil's grip began to cease
No longer seeking others' grace
She found her worth in her own space
From a maze of doubts to paths well-trod
She learned to trust the voice of God
No longer bound by past mistakes
Her spirit healed, her soul awake
From tears that flowed like rivers wide
To flames of passion, burning inside

Her fragility transformed into steel
A warrior's heart, with wounds that healed
From timid steps to strides so bold
Her story is written, alas untold
No longer chained by what has been
She stands unbroken, fierce and keen
From ashes of despair to skies above
She found the strength to rise and love
No longer a prisoner to her pain
She danced in freedom's gentle rain
From broken heart to mended soul
Her journey's made her truly whole
A girl once lost, now found her way
And in her light, she'll always choose to stay

From the ashes I rise ...

GET IN TOUCH WITH THE AUTHOR

Email: tarjanigajjar18@gmail.com